How Many Seconds?

by Katherine Krieg

Say Hello to Amicus Readers.

You'll find our helpful dog, Amicus, chasing a ball—to let you know the reading level of a book.

1

Learn to Read

Frequent repetition, high frequency words, and close photo-text matches introduce familiar topics and provide ample support for brand new readers.

2

Read Independently

Some repetition is mixed with varied sentence structures and a select amount of new vocabulary words are introduced with text and photo support.

3

Read to Know More

Interesting facts and engaging art and photos give fluent readers fun books both for reading practice and to learn about new topics.

Amicus Readers are published by Amicus
P.O. Box 1329, Mankato, MN 56002
www.amicuspublishing.us

Photo Credits: Patrick Foto/Shutterstock Images, cover; iStockphoto, 1; Shutterstock Images, 3, 14–15, 16 (top); Jean Schweitzer/Thinkstock, 4–5; Rosalie Kreulen/Shutterstock Images, 6–7; David Ocrea/ Shutterstock Images, 8–9; Ami Parikh/Shutterstock Images, 10; Vuttichai Chaiya/Shutterstock Images, 13; Africa Studio/Shutterstock Images, 16 (bottom)

Produced for Amicus by The Peterson Publishing Company and Red Line Editorial.

Editor Jenna Gleisner
Designer Becky Daum

Library of Congress
Cataloging-in-Publication Data
Krieg, Katherine, author.
    How many seconds? / by Katherine Krieg.
        pages cm. -- (Measuring time) (Amicus readers)
    Summary: "Introduces activities young readers experience in a matter of seconds, such as sneezing or picking a flower, while teaching ways to measure seconds and how they compare to minutes."-- Provided by publisher.
    Audience: K to grade 3
    ISBN 978-1-60753-720-5 (library binding)
    ISBN 978-1-60753-824-0 (ebook)
    1. Time measurements--Juvenile literature. 2. Time--Juvenile literature. I. Title.
    QB213.K74 2014
    529.7--dc23
                                    2014048093

Printed in Malaysia
10 9 8 7 6 5 4 3 2 1

We use seconds to measure time. A second is very short. It takes about 1 second to sneeze. What can you do in 1 second at the park?

Ava picks a flower at the park. It takes

1 second

to pluck it from the ground.

Kai watches a hummingbird.
The hummingbird flaps its
wings 50 times in
1 second.

Jose goes down the slide. He measures how long it takes. His stopwatch shows it takes **5 seconds** to reach the bottom.

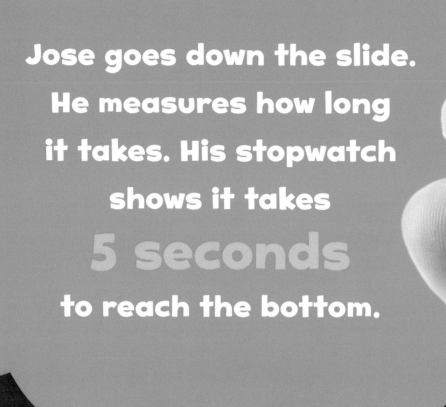

Sam crosses on the monkey bars. Sophia times the seconds with a stopwatch. Sam crosses in **30 seconds.**

It takes Sophia

60 seconds

to run across the park.
The second hand on her
watch makes a full circle.
That is 1 minute.

second hand

13

There are lots of fun things at the park that only take a few seconds.

What can you do in seconds?

15

Measuring Seconds

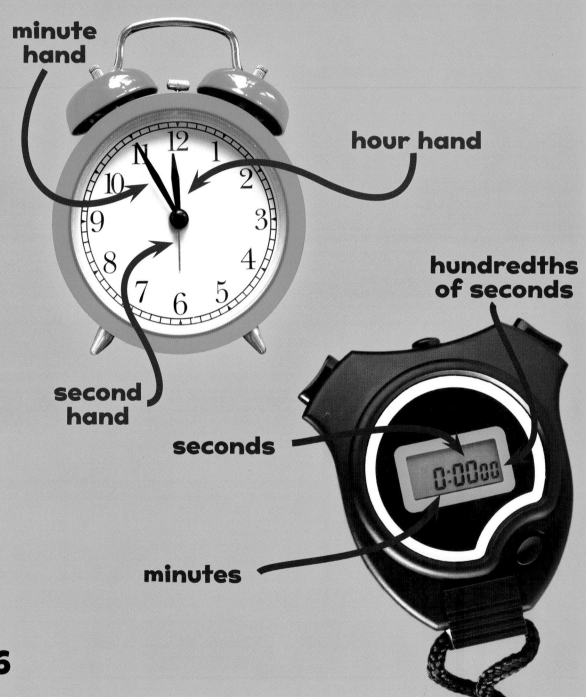

minute hand

hour hand

second hand

hundredths of seconds

seconds

minutes

0:00:00